WHERE DID SACAGAWEA JOIN THE CORPS OF DISCOVERY?

And Other Questions about the Lewis and Clark Expedition

Linda Gondosch

LERNER PUBLICATIONS · MINNEAPOLIS

A Word about Language

English word usage, spelling, grammar, and punctuation have changed over the centuries. We have preserved original spellings and word usage in the quotations included in this book.

Lerner Publications Company
A division of Lerner Publishing Group, Inc.
241 First Avenue North
Minneapolis, MN 55401 USA

For reading levels and more information, look up this title at www.lernerbooks.com.

Library of Congress Cataloging-in-Publication Data

Gondosch, Linda.
    Where did Sacagawea join the Corps of Discovery?: and other questions about the Lewis and Clark expedition / by Linda Gondosch.
        p.   cm. — (Six questions of American history)
    Includes bibliographical references and index.
    ISBN 978-0-7613-5226-6 (lib. bdg. : alk. paper)
    ISBN 978-0-7613-7237-0 (EB pdf)
    1. Lewis and Clark Expedition (1804–1806)—Juvenile literature. 2. West (U.S.)—Discovery and exploration—Juvenile literature. 3. West (U.S.)—Description and travel—Juvenile literature. 4. Lewis, Meriwether, 1774–1809—Juvenile literature. 5. Clark, William, 1770–1838—Juvenile literature. 6. Explorers—West (U.S.)—Biography—Juvenile literature. I. Title.
    F592.7.G66 2011
    917.804'2—dc22   2010007068

Manufactured in the United States of America
2-38781-10881-6/3/2016

TABLE OF CONTENTS

.... 4

THE SIX
QUESTIONS
HELP YOU
DISCOVER THE
FACTS!

INTRODUCTION

On May 14, 1804, about forty men boarded a 55-foot (17-meter) covered, flat-bottomed boat and two large canoes. They were eager to begin their adventure! The three boats left Saint Louis in the modern-day state of Missouri. They slowly moved up the Missouri River. Mosquitoes and gnats bit the men's arms and flew into their eyes.

This band of men was headed into Louisiana Territory, an area that stretched from the Mississippi River to the Rocky Mountains. The area was unexplored. It wasn't even shown on a map.

For many years, French traders and British explorers had traveled into Louisiana. They had brought back stories about the Rocky Mountains. The men had heard wild tales about monstrous bears, woolly mammoths, giant sloths, dinosaur bones, volcanoes, and mountains of pure salt.

What would they find? Dangerous rapids? Poisonous snakes? Hungry wolves? They were almost sure to meet some unfriendly— even hostile—Indians. There was a chance these men would never return.

Lewis and Clark canoed down this area of the Columbia River during their exploration.

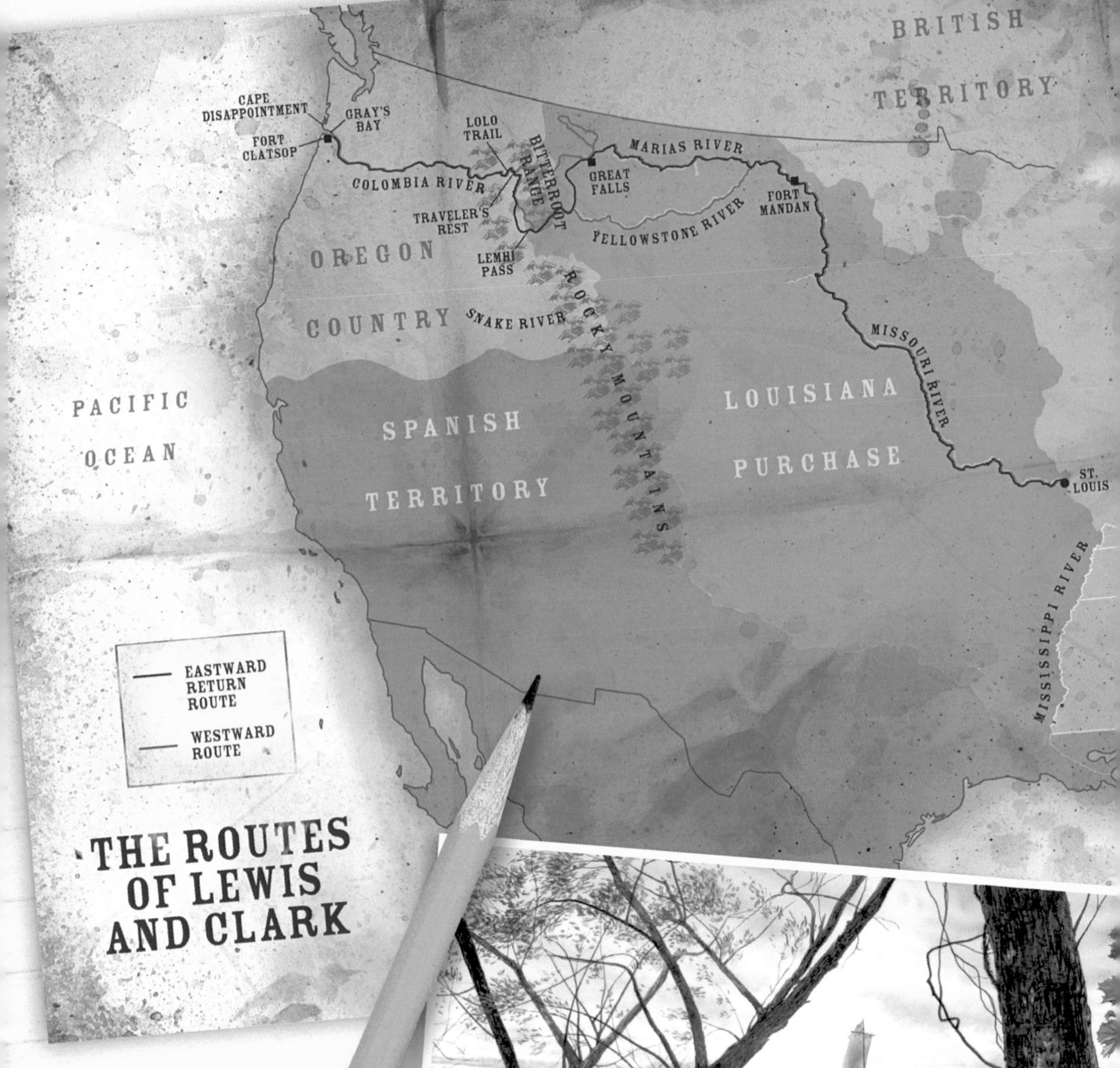

THE ROUTES OF LEWIS AND CLARK

BRITISH TERRITORY

CAPE DISAPPOINTMENT

GRAY'S BAY

FORT CLATSOP

LOLO TRAIL

MARIAS RIVER

GREAT FALLS

BITTERROOT RANGE

COLOMBIA RIVER

TRAVELER'S REST

FORT MANDAN

OREGON

YELLOWSTONE RIVER

LEMHI PASS

COUNTRY

SNAKE RIVER

ROCKY MOUNTAINS

MISSOURI RIVER

PACIFIC

OCEAN

SPANISH

TERRITORY

LOUISIANA

PURCHASE

ST. LOUIS

MISSISSIPPI RIVER

EASTWARD RETURN ROUTE

WESTWARD ROUTE

This modern painting by Michael Haynes shows the men leaving Saint Louis to explore the Louisiana Territory on May 14, 1804.

Lewis and Clark say their good-byes to friends and family in this painting by Michael Haynes.

ONE THE VOYAGE OF DISCOVERY BEGINS

In 1801, when Thomas Jefferson became the third U.S. president, most Americans lived within 50 miles (80 kilometers) of the Atlantic Ocean. By 1803 the country's western boundary was the Mississippi River.

France had gained control of Louisiana Territory, or simply Louisiana, in 1800. Great Britain held land along the territory's northern border, and Spain held land to the southwest. But President Jefferson wanted Louisiana for the United States. He dreamed of a vast "Empire of Liberty" that would someday stretch from the Atlantic Ocean all the way west to the Pacific Ocean.

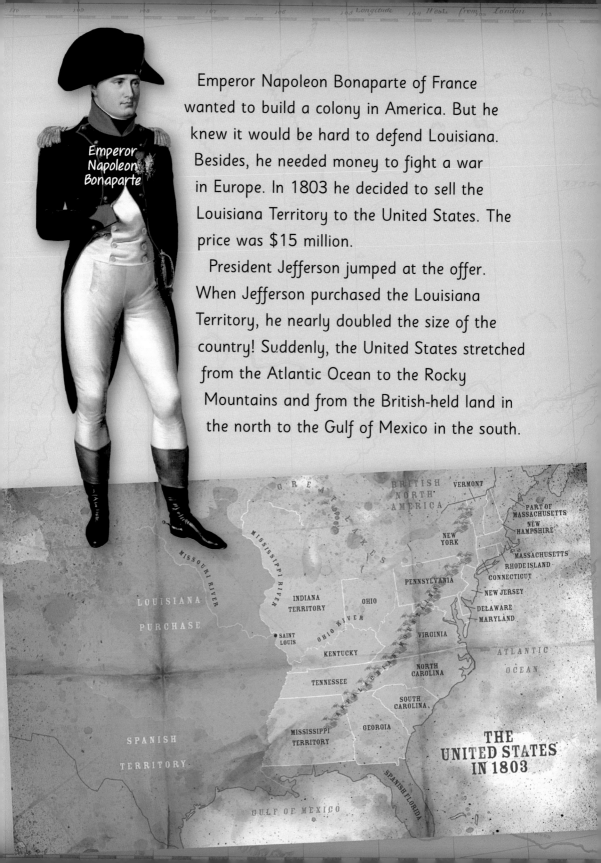

Emperor Napoleon Bonaparte

Emperor Napoleon Bonaparte of France wanted to build a colony in America. But he knew it would be hard to defend Louisiana. Besides, he needed money to fight a war in Europe. In 1803 he decided to sell the Louisiana Territory to the United States. The price was $15 million.

President Jefferson jumped at the offer. When Jefferson purchased the Louisiana Territory, he nearly doubled the size of the country! Suddenly, the United States stretched from the Atlantic Ocean to the Rocky Mountains and from the British-held land in the north to the Gulf of Mexico in the south.

THE
UNITED STATES
IN 1803

Jefferson had always planned on sending an army expedition into the West. But after the Louisiana Purchase, the expedition would be exploring mainly U.S. land. Jefferson hoped to find a water route— later called the Northwest Passage—through the country. To reach the Pacific Ocean, traders had to travel very long distances. If Americans could find a river route across North America, they would shorten travel time. They would give traders a quicker way to reach markets in Asia.

> a journey undertaken for a specific purpose

The president also wanted the explorers to bring back scientific information about the land. He wanted to learn about the climate, the soil, minerals, animals, and plants. He wanted maps drawn of the mountains and the rivers. He wanted information about the Indians of the West and their languages, their customs, and their potential for trade.

The president chose his private secretary, Meriwether Lewis, to lead the expedition. "The object of your mission is to explore the Missouri river . . . [to find] the most direct . . . water communication across this continent for the purposes of commerce." In other words, he told them to find the Northwest Passage.

> "The object of your mission is to explore the Missouri river."

President Thomas Jefferson

SHOPPING FOR SUPPLIES

Lewis and Clark needed many supplies for the expedition. These included axes, rifles, gunpowder, knives, fishing hooks, and pipe tomahawks (special pipes that had tomahawk handles and were smoked with the Indians). The captains bought scientific instruments, compasses, ink and paper, mosquito netting, books, copper kettles, salt, dried soup, candles, and portable desks. They also collected gifts—such as beads, scissors, mirrors, ribbons, silk handkerchiefs, ear trinkets, and corn grinders—for the Indians.

Lewis had been a soldier in the U.S. Army. He was an expert hunter and frontiersman, but he wanted help. He asked his army friend William Clark to join him as co-captain of the expedition. They had a keelboat built. They bought two pirogues—large, flat-bottomed canoes with sails.

keelboat a covered, flat-bottomed riverboat that is usually rowed poled, or towed

The two captains spent months collecting supplies and choosing strong, young men to explore the West with them. They chose soldiers, boatmen, and hunters. Among the volunteers were a gunsmith, a blacksmith, a carpenter, a miller, a tailor, and an interpreter. Clark also brought his slave, York. When the group returned, each of the men, except York, was to be given 320 acres (130 hectares) of land. President Jefferson called the group the Corps of Discovery.

interpreter A person who translates other languages

Corps an organized group of people having a common activity

The Lewis and Clark Expedition started up the Missouri River from the modern-day state of Missouri. The men were often sick with dysentery (diarrhea), caused by drinking muddy river water. At first, the expedition saw few Indians. Then they reached the villages of the Otos and the Missouris. The Indians who lived there were hunting buffalo on the plains.

SEAMAN

Meriwether Lewis brought Seaman, his large black Newfoundland dog, on the expedition. Seaman was an excellent watchdog that barked at bears and wolves to scare them away. He also proved helpful by catching squirrels and beavers. Seaman could usually be found trotting beside Captain Lewis. The dog traveled thousands of miles, most of the time on foot.

On August 3, Captain Lewis and Captain Clark held their first Indian council near modern-day Council Bluffs, Iowa. The uniformed soldiers drilled and paraded past the Indians. The soldiers fired their rifles and shot their swivel cannon. Lewis gave a speech. He told the Indians that he had come from seventeen great "nations" (states) and that President Thomas Jefferson was their Great Father.

Captains Meriwether Lewis and William Clark hold a council with the Indians at Council Bluffs, Iowa, in this artwork from the book *Journal of Voyages* written by Corps of Discovery member Patrick Gass in 1811.

Lewis and Clark gave these Jefferson peace medals to the Indians.

The Great Father wanted peace among the tribes. Lewis said that the United States wanted to trade with them and have friendly relations. He discouraged them from trading with the Spanish and the French.

Lewis then gave the Indians presents—combs, red face paint, gunpowder, bullets, and silver peace medals. These medals had a picture of President Jefferson on one side. The other side showed a handshake with the words *PEACE AND FRIENDSHIP.* The Otos and Missouris listened politely and seemed pleased with their gifts.

NEXT QUESTION

WHO WERE THE INDIANS THAT CLARK CALLED THE PIRATES OF THE MISSOURI RIVER?

TWO INDIANS, BUFFALO, AND PRAIRIE DOGS

Since Captain Clark was the better navigator, he usually stayed on the keelboat. He carefully charted the river's course and drew maps of the land. He used a compass mounted on the boat. Captain Lewis liked to walk along the shore. He gathered samples of plants and studied the local animals. President Jefferson had ordered Lewis to carefully describe in writing anything new to science.

When the expedition reached the Great Plains, Lewis and Clark found much to write in their journals. The grasslands were filled with plants and animals. Many were unknown in the eastern United States. Elk, deer, beavers, wild

one who steers or manages (a boat) in sailing

the broad level land that stretches east from the base of the Rocky Mountains for about 400 miles (644 kilmeters)

12

turkeys, pronghorn antelope, jackrabbits, and buffalo roamed the plains. "I do not think I exagerate when I estimate the number of Buffaloe which could be [seen] at one view to amount to 3000," Lewis wrote. He also described the plants, including purple prairie clover, buffalo berry, and snakeweed.

One day Joseph Field, a soldier from Kentucky, killed a buffalo. The men dined on buffalo hump, buffalo tongue, and buffalo steak. They were so hungry that each one ate about 9 pounds (4 kilograms) of meat!

On September 7, a group of prairie dogs surprised them. The Corps wanted to send a real, live prairie dog to President Jefferson. They poured buckets of water down a hole. Out popped a prairie dog. They caught it and put it in a cage. They planned to send it all the way to Washington, D.C.

Toward the end of September, the expedition reached the villages of the Teton Sioux Indians. The Teton Sioux often demanded huge payments from strangers in their territory. They wanted complete control of trade in their land—with no competition.

"I do not think I exagerate when I estimate the number of Buffaloe which could be [seen] at one view to amount to 3000."

Captain Meriwether Lewis

In this 1830s artwork by George Catlin, the Teton Sioux hold a council.

Lewis and Clark had a council with three chiefs—Black Buffalo, the Partisan, and Buffalo Medicine. Sioux warriors stood nearby. After Lewis's speech about friendly trade with the seventeen great nations of the United States, he presented gifts to the chiefs. But the Indians grumbled. They wanted more. Three warriors grabbed the towline of the pirogue. Another grabbed the mast. They demanded to keep the large canoe if they did not get more gifts.

mast: a long pole rising from the deck of a ship and supporting smaller poles, rigging, and sails

Clark raised his sword. He refused to be bullied by the Sioux Indians. Lewis prepared to fire the swivel cannon mounted on the keelboat. Members of the Corps of Discovery raised their rifles. The warriors lifted their bows. At the last minute, Black Buffalo ordered his warriors to release the towline and the mast. Guns and bows were lowered. The Corps of Discovery managed to escape the Teton Sioux after giving them more tobacco. Clark was bitter about giving up the extra supplies. He called the Teton Sioux "the pirates of the Missouri."

The autumn air grew chilly. Canadian geese, snow geese, and ducks flew overhead. Lewis and Clark noted and described them in their journals. Some of the other corps members—Patrick Gass, Joseph Whitehouse, John Ordway, and Charles Floyd—also kept journals.

By October the expedition had reached the Mandan Indian villages in modern-day North Dakota. The Mandan and nearby Hidatsa villages were a trading center for fur traders from as far away as Canada. These villages were the last western landmark on any map.

A view of a Mandan village is depicted in this 1833 painting by Karl Bodmer.

It was time to build winter quarters. On November 3, work began on Fort Mandan. The men built a wooden stockade across the river from one of the Mandan villages. The next day, Lewis met a French Canadian fur trader named Toussaint Charbonneau. He lived with the Hidatsas. Since Charbonneau knew the Hidatsa language as well as French, Lewis hired him as another interpreter for the journey. Charbonneau was also a good cook. (The men especially loved his tasty buffalo sausages!) Charbonneau brought along his wife, a sixteen-year-old Shoshone Indian named Sacagawea. She was six months pregnant.

The river froze and temperatures dropped below 0°F (−18°C) that winter. But New Year's Day of 1805 found the Corps of Discovery inside a Mandan dome-shaped, earthen lodge, partying with the Indians. Pierre Cruzatte, an expedition member, played his fiddle while his friends danced. The Mandans were fascinated by Clark's servant, York. They had never seen a black man. One chief even rubbed York's skin to see if he was covered with paint.

In February Sacagawea gave birth to a baby boy.

THE BUFFALO HUNT

On December 7, Chief Big White invited Lewis, Clark, and fifteen men to go on a buffalo hunt. Clark was impressed by how the Indians rode bareback at great speeds, guiding their horses with their legs while shooting arrows. The American guests killed fourteen buffalo in one day. This time they ate only the buffalo tongues. Wolves ate the rest. The temperature dropped to below 0°F (−18°C), but the men wanted to stay with the Mandans to hunt the next day.

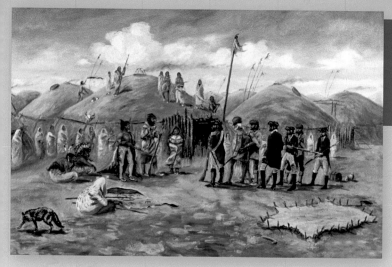

This painting by Vern Erickson created in 1963 shows the captains making plans with Charbonneau and Sacagawea at the Hidatsa village.

His parents named him Jean-Baptiste Charbonneau. But Clark called him Pomp, which means "Little Chief" in the Shoshone language. Little Pomp became the youngest member of the Lewis and Clark Expedition.

At Fort Mandan, the men worked hard all winter. They hunted, traded with the Indians, repaired equipment, and built more canoes. Lewis and Clark wrote reports to President Jefferson, describing everything they had seen and done.

They also planned the next part of their journey. They asked the Mandans about the mountains and rivers of the West. The Indians told them about a great waterfall on the Missouri River. The Mandans informed them of the Shoshone Indians who owned many horses. And they warned Lewis and Clark of dangers ahead.

NEXT QUESTION

WHERE WOULD THEY MEET THE DANGERS THE MANDANS DESCRIBED?

This painting by John Clymer (1907-1989) shows a large grizzly bear chasing two Corps of Discovery men into a canoe.

THREE WILD AND DANGEROUS ADVENTURES

As spring came, the snow began to melt. On April 7, 1805, Lewis and Clark sent the keelboat and several men back to Saint Louis with maps and reports for President Jefferson. They packed the boat with soil and plant samples, seeds, Indian artifacts, animal skins, letters, and more. Six caged animals traveled on the boat. These included the prairie dog, a grouse hen, and four magpies (a type of bird).

usually handmade objects (as tools or ornaments) representing a particular culture

The rest of the Corps of Discovery headed upriver into unknown territory in two pirogues and six canoes. They were beyond any known map. Which way would the river turn? How high were the mountains? What Indians would they meet?

In May six men spotted a huge grizzly bear and shot it. They wounded the animal but didn't kill it. The angry bear chased two of the men to the riverbank. They jumped 20 feet (6 m) to the water below. With a roar, the bear jumped in after them. The bear almost reached one of the swimmers when another man shot it dead.

That same afternoon, Charbonneau was riding in one of the pirogues. Sacagawea and three-month-old Pomp rode with him. The wind began to gust, and Charbonneau lost control of the boat. It began to tilt and fill with water! Frantic, Captain Lewis watched from shore as valuable articles, such as journals, medicines, scientific instruments, maps, and more, fell into the river. Fortunately, Sacagawea stayed calm. She reached out and saved many floating items, including the priceless journals.

A few weeks later, a bull (male) buffalo charged through the campground as the men lay sleeping. The buffalo stormed back and forth.

Sacagawea carries Pomp in a Shoshone-style cradleboard in the spring of 1805 in this artwork by Michael Haynes.

In this painting by Michael Haynes, Louis and Clark reach a fork in the Missouri River.

His hooves pounded within inches of the men's heads. Lewis's dog, Seaman, barked loudly until the buffalo ran away. The men did not sleep much after that!

In June the Corps of Discovery reached a fork in the river. Which branch should they take? The captains thought that the south fork was the true Missouri River. Everyone else insisted the Missouri branched northward. After scouting around, the Corps agreed to follow the captains up the south fork. Lewis wrote in his journal, "They said very cheerfully that they were ready to follow us any wher we thought proper to direct but that they still thought that the other was the river." By this time, the men had complete trust in their leaders.

When the explorers reached a thundering, 90-foot-high (27 m) waterfall, they knew the captains had chosen the right fork. They named it the Great Falls of the Missouri. But instead of one waterfall, there were five! The men buried some of their baggage. Then they portaged canoes and cargo

carried boats and goods overland

around the falls. They thought it would take one week to portage around the falls. Instead, it took one month.

Farther on, the Missouri River grew smaller and turned into a shallow stream. They had reached the Rocky Mountains and could go no farther by canoe. Captain Lewis hiked ahead with a few men and searched for the Shoshone Indians. They desperately needed horses from the Shoshones to travel over the mountains.

THE PORTAGE AROUND THE GREAT FALLS

The portage around the Great Falls of the Missouri was extremely hard. The men hid a pirogue and buried some of their heaviest cargo so their supplies would be safe until their return trip. They built wagons to carry the rest of their baggage almost 20 miles (32 km) around the five waterfalls. Some days were miserably hot. Other days brought thunderstorms with hailstones as large as apples. And their moccasins were shredded after stepping on prickly pear cactus that grew there.

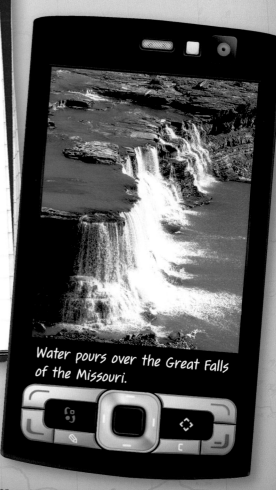

Water pours over the Great Falls of the Missouri.

On August 12, after an uphill hike in modern-day Montana, Lewis and his group reached a high ridge on the Continental Divide. (The point was later named Lemhi Pass.) They followed a rippling stream to where it flowed from a spring. They had finally reached the beginning of the great Missouri River. Lewis called it "the most distant fountain of the waters of the mighty Missouri."

But when he climbed farther and looked out over the mountains, his heart sank. Captain Lewis had hoped to see low-lying plains with a river flowing toward the Pacific Ocean. Instead, he

CROSSING THE CONTINENTAL DIVIDE

As they crossed the Continental Divide, the Corps of Discovery left the United States and entered Oregon Country. Great Britain, France, Russia, and Spain had already tried to claim Oregon Country. But President Jefferson hoped the Lewis and Clark Expedition would give the United States a stronger claim.

Lewis at the Continental Divide

saw "immence ranges of high mountains still to the West. . . with their tops partially covered with snow." There were more mountains than he had ever imagined. On Lemhi Pass, Captain Lewis realized the dream of a Northwest Passage had finally died. There would be no easy passage over these mountains.

Fortunately, Lewis and part of the Corps soon found the Shoshone Indians. Using sign language (hand and body motions), the captain tried to explain the expedition. But the Shoshones were suspicious of these strangers. After all, they might be enemies. Despite suspicions, Chief Cameahwait and his warriors agreed to meet the rest of the Corps of Discovery.

Captain Lewis led the Indians back to the expedition's campground. Neither Lewis nor Clark could speak the Shoshone language. But Sacagawea had been kidnapped from the Shoshones as a child. She could interpret. The captains told her to ask Chief Cameahwait for horses so the expedition could cross the mountains.

WHAT IS OREGON COUNTRY?

Oregon Country is the northwestern portion of North America that was not yet part of the United States. This part later became the states of Oregon, Washington, and Idaho.

During these talks, Sacagawea suddenly realized that Cameahwait was her brother, whom she had not seen for many years. Sacagawea and Cameahwait had a joyful reunion! No longer suspicious, Cameahwait gladly sold several horses to the captains. They gave the name Camp Fortunate to the place where the Corps of Discovery met the Shoshones.

By the end of August, the Corps had purchased twenty-nine horses and three colts. The captains hired a Shoshone named Old Toby to guide the expedition across the mountains. They followed an Indian trail northward. After a few days, Old Toby lost the trail. By the time he found it again, snow was falling. They found little to eat. They made do with the dried soup that Lewis had purchased in Saint Louis. But the soup tasted so bad that they killed a colt and ate it.

In this painting by Michael Haynes, Sacagawea shows Pomp to her long-lost brother, Cameahwait.

Members of the Corps struggle across the Bitterroot Mountains in this painting by John Clymer.

The travelers grew colder, wetter, and hungrier.

a part of the Rocky Mountain range

On September 11, 1805, they turned westward and started across the snow-peaked Bitterroot Mountains. By this time, some men had no shoes or socks. They tied rags around their feet and trudged on. Patrick Gass, a sergeant in the Corps of Discovery, wrote that they "proceeded over the most terrible mountains I ever beheld."

Captain Clark wrote, "I could observe high ruged mountains in every direction as far as I could see." By September 17, the explorers were starving. They killed another colt and ate it.

NEXT QUESTION

WHEN WOULD THE EXPEDITION REACH THE PACIFIC OCEAN?

Two corpsmen *(right)* look off into the distance next to a Nez Perce Indian *(left)*. The painting was done by Roger Cooke in 2003.

FOUR WINTER AT FORT CLATSOP

Normally, it took six days to cross the Bitterroot Mountains. But the Corps of Discovery needed eleven days. Weak from starvation, the expedition members stumbled out of the Rocky Mountains and into the Indian village of the Nez Perce. Chief Twisted Hair and his warriors knew they could kill these weakened white men. They could easily take their goods, including their guns.

However, an old Nez Perce woman named Watkuweis begged Twisted Hair, "Do them no hurt." Watkuweis remembered being treated well by white people after she had escaped from another tribe. Because of Watkuweis, Twisted Hair spared the lives of the Corps of Discovery.

The Nez Perce gave the hungry men and Sacagawea camas roots and salmon to eat. (There were no buffalo west of the Rockies.) The Nez Perce taught them how to burn out ponderosa pine logs for canoes. They even offered to care for their horses while the expedition traveled on by canoe.

After Corps members regained their strength, they left the Nez Perce and canoed down the Clearwater River. Paddling with the current—instead of against it, as they had been doing—was much easier. After a while, however, the Clearwater River turned into the dangerous Snake River. The water rushed through narrow canyons and rocky rapids.

camas roots the edible bul (or roots) of lily plants

ponderosa pine a tall timber tree of weste North Americ with long needles

current river water moving continuously in a certain direction

The Corps of Discovery canoes through the rapids on the Snake River in this 2003 painting by Roger Cooke.

By October 1805, the Corps of Discovery had become impatient. They wanted to reach the ocean before winter trapped them inland. Instead of portaging around, they shot through one rapid after another. Canoes spun around as they crashed into rocks. One canoe hit a rock, split open, and sank—losing much valuable equipment. It was more than Old Toby, their Shoshone guide, could take. He ran off, stopping only to pick up two of the expedition's horses.

The Snake River emptied into the Columbia River, near the home of the Chinook Indians. The Chinooks gathered to see whether the white men would drown as they plunged down the rapids. Afterward, Captain Clark was glad to write, "We passed Safe to the astonishment of all the [Indians] . . . who viewed us from the top of the rock."

On November 7, Clark wrote, "Ocian in view! O! the joy." It was really Gray's Bay, an inlet of the sea 20 miles (32 km) from the ocean. Waves rolled in from the ocean. The weather grew bad. The whole group was stuck in a rainy, windy cove for days. Not until November 15 did they reach the mouth

"Ocian in view! O! the joy."

Captain William Clark

In this painting by Michael Haynes, the Corps of Discovery is trapped in the wind and the rain on the shore of Gray's Bay.

WHERE IS GRAY'S BAY?
Gray's Bay is on the Washington side of the Columbia River. It is about 20 miles (32 km) from the Pacific Ocean.

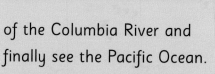

of the Columbia River and finally see the Pacific Ocean.

When the storms ended, Lewis and Clark explored the beach. They searched the horizon for a trading ship. They hoped to send some men home by ship, along with some journals.

But they didn't see any ship nor did they even know for sure that one would come. Captain Clark carved into a tree "Capt William Clark December 3rd 1805. By Land. U States in 1804 & 1805." They called it Cape Disappointment because they found no white settlers, no trading post, and no passing ships.

The captains decided to set up camp near the ocean. But should they camp near the Chinook Indians on the north side of the river or near the Clatsop Indians on the south side? They put it to a vote. Everyone voted, even York and Sacagawea. They chose to stay near the Clatsops, where there were more elks for food.

The weary travelers began building Fort Clatsop in early December. They moved in on

A replica of Lewis and Clark's post at Fort Clatsop is displayed at the Fort Clatsop National Memorial in Oregon.

December 23. What a miserable Christmas! They ate spoiled elk and stale, dried fish for dinner while rain beat on the roof. (During their three-month stay at Fort Clatsop, only twelve days had no rain.)

At Fort Clatsop, hunters killed 131 elks, twenty deer, a few beavers, some otters, and one raccoon. One group boiled kettles of seawater to make salt for their meat. Other than hunting, making salt, and smoking meat, the men stayed busy stitching 338 pairs of new moccasins, making clothes, and repairing equipment.

This artwork depicts Lewis, Clark, and Sacagawea as they visit with the Clatsop Indians at Fort Clatsop in 1805.

Lewis collected this huckleberry branch at Fort Clatsop on January 27, 1806.

Captain Clark finished his 4-foot-wide (1 m) map of the land from Fort Mandan to the western coastline. He figured they had journeyed 4,162 miles (6,698 km) from Saint Louis to the Pacific Ocean. Captain Lewis wrote descriptions and drew pictures of hundreds of animals and plants. He wrote about ferns, mosses, bilberries, and huckleberries near the fort. He described the Chinook Indians, their excellent canoes, and their wooden houses.

The group was wet and cold and plagued with fleas. Many were sick with colds and flu. Would winter never end? The Clatsop Indians visited now and then, bringing dried fish, roots, and dogs to eat. But the men were homesick and bored. They wanted to go home. President Jefferson was waiting to hear about their adventures. He was especially eager to learn whether the expedition had found a Northwest Passage.

THE DOG EATERS

The Pacific Coast Indians lived mainly on salmon and camas roots. The men of the expedition became very sick when they first ate the fish and roots diet. They were not used to it. They had always eaten red meat, so they bought dogs from the Indians and mainly ate dog meat. The Indians thought such a diet was horrible. They mockingly called the white men "dog eaters." They sold them hundreds of dogs anyway, and many men of the expedition thought they were "tasty."

NEXT QUESTION

WHAT WOULD AMERICANS LEARN FROM THE LEWIS AND CLARK EXPEDITION?

The Corps of Discovery paddles up the Columbia River in this painting by Roger Cooke done in 2003.

FIVE ESCAPE FROM THE BLACKFEET

On March 23, 1806, the Corps of Discovery gladly left Fort Clatsop. They gave the fort to the Indians and paddled upriver. The group began their journey back across the North American continent. But Lewis was worried. He had only two handkerchief bundles of their remaining Indian gifts.

The expedition was not sorry to leave the Chinook Indians. The Chinooks had wanted high prices for items the men needed. Worst of all, the Chinooks had stolen things whenever they could.

As the expedition journeyed up the Columbia River, the Indians continued to steal. They took a tomahawk, an ax, a saddle, and a robe. When they stole Seaman, Lewis demanded they return his dog. After a long chase, the Indians finally returned Seaman.

By May the expedition had reached the Nez Perce Indians. The horses were still there, waiting to carry the Corps of Discovery back over the treacherous mountains. The Nez Perce, however, warned them that it was too early to cross the mountains. They would have to wait until late June. Captain Lewis must have thought of his home in Virginia. On May 17, 1806, he wrote in his journal about "the mountains; that icy barier which seperates me from my friends and Country, from all which makes life [worthwhile] patience, patience." The Rocky Mountains seemed like a wall, keeping them from traveling on.

This 2003 Roger Cooke painting depicts the Corps of Discovery campsite in May. In the center is Sacagawea and Pomp.

Corps members passed the time by playing games and holding tournaments with the friendly Nez Perce. Foot races, shooting matches, horse races, and games helped the men stay physically fit.

Finally, on June 15, the Corps of Discovery set out to cross the Bitterroot mountain range. The Indians warned that it was too early, and they were right. Within three days, the Corps ran into 15 feet (5 m) of snow. They turned back.

A week later, with three Nez Perce guides, they tried again. First, the guides set fire to a grove of fir trees that lit up like fireworks. They did this "to bring fair weather for our journey," explained Clark. This time they crossed the mountains in six days and arrived at a place called Traveler's Rest.

But the captains were not finished exploring. Instead of heading east, Lewis split the Corps into smaller groups. Captain Clark took Sacagawea and several men down the Yellowstone River to explore. Captain Lewis took the rest

POMPY'S TOWER

While Lewis's group explored the Marias River, Clark and the others traveled down the Yellowstone River. Clark's group discovered a 150-foot (46 m) sandstone butte, an isolated hill with steep sides, filled with old Indian petroglyphs. Petroglyphs are pictures carved into rock. Clark named the butte Pompy's Tower in honor of Sacagawea's son, Pomp. Clark wrote on the tower, "W. Clark July 25, 1806." His signature is the only remaining physical evidence of the Lewis and Clark Expedition to be found along the trail. In 1814 Pompy's Tower was renamed Pompey's Pillar. In 2001 Pompey's Pillar became a national monument.

back to the Great Falls. From there Lewis, George Drouillard, and Joseph and Reuben Field rode on horseback along the Marias River. Lewis wanted to find the northern source of the Marias tributary. Louisiana Territory included all land drained by the Missouri River and its tributaries. If Lewis could find the source of the Marias River, that would show how far north Louisiana extended.

a stream feeding a larger body of water

On their way back, Lewis and his men ran into eight Blackfeet warriors. The cautious explorers knew the Blackfeet were as dangerous as the Sioux. Trying to act unafraid, Lewis talked with the Indians using sign language. The men even camped with the Blackfeet that night.

Early the next morning, a Blackfoot tried to steal Reuben Field's gun. Field stabbed him to death. Captain Lewis shot and killed another Blackfoot as more warriors tried to steal his rifle and all the horses. It was the only time during the journey that expedition members killed anyone.

BRITISH TERRITORY

POINTS OF
SEPARATION AND
REUNION

CAMP
DISAPPOINTMENT

FIGHT WITH BLACKFEET

MARIAS RIVER

PACIFIC
OCEAN

TRAVELER'S
REST

MISSOURI RIVER

GREAT
FALLS

POINT OF
REUNION

CLARK'S
EXPLORATION

BITTERROOT
RIVER

THREE
FORKS OF THE
MISSOURI

LEWIS'S
EXPLORATION

JEFFERSON
RIVER

YELLOWSTONE RIVER

OREGON COUNTRY

LOUISIANA

PURCHASE

SPANISH TERRITORY

Knowing the entire Blackfeet tribe would soon come looking for them, Captain Lewis and his men rode as fast as they could all day and all night. They rode through thunder, lightning, and pouring rain. Finally, they met the rest of the expedition at the Missouri River. Moving from horses to canoes, they paddled downriver—this time with the current. They felt as if they were speeding through the water at 7 miles (11 km) per hour, leaving the angry Blackfeet far behind.

One day, weeks later, Captain Lewis and Pierre Cruzatte stopped to hunt for food. Lewis was about to shoot an elk when suddenly Cruzatte shot him in the rear end! (Cruzatte was nearsighted in one eye and blind in the other.) For much of the remaining journey, Captain Lewis had to lie on his stomach in the pirogue under the hot summer sun.

When the expedition reached the Mandan villages, it received bad news. Many Indian tribes were at war.

The Blackfeet set up camp in this painting by W. Langdon Kihn from the 1940s.

The Arikaras were fighting the Mandans. The Hidatsas were fighting the Shoshones, and the Sioux had raided the Mandan villages. Lewis's speeches to the Indians about peace had not changed things.

At Fort Mandan, Toussaint Charbonneau bid farewell to the Corps of Discovery. He returned to the Hidatsa village with Sacagawea and eighteen-month-old Pomp. Saying good-bye was sad. John Colter, an expedition member, also left the group to join some fur trappers headed west. Colter had no interest in returning to civilization.

As some people were lost, others were gained. Chief Big White agreed to travel with the expedition downriver to Saint Louis and on to Washington, D.C., to meet President Jefferson. The chief brought his wife and son with him.

On the water, the men began paddling faster. They were eager to see their families again. The Corps met more fur trappers canoeing upriver. The trappers were shocked to see the Corps of Discovery. Most Americans had given them up for dead, the trappers said.

THE BLACKFEET AND THE BUFFALO

The Blackfeet Indians were buffalo hunters. They used almost every part of the animal. They ate the meat or dried it to eat later. They used buffalo hides, or skins, to make moccasins, robes, and other clothing. They hung hides over log poles to form houses called tepees. The Blackfeet used buffalo fat to make soap. Bones were carved into tools and sewing needles. The buffalo's stomach and bladder became handy containers to hold things. They even used buffalo manure as fuel for fires.

Lewis's Newfoundland, Seaman, jumps toward the shore of Saint Louis as the Corps of Discovery arrives home in this painting by Michael Haynes.

On September 23, 1806, the Lewis and Clark Expedition reached Saint Louis. The entire population of one thousand crowded the riverbank! People cheered and fired guns.

Of course, President Jefferson would be disappointed to learn that there was no easy river route across the United States, no Northwest Passage. But the two-and-one-half-year expedition provided a wealth of information about the American West. Lewis and Clark brought home excellent maps of the Louisiana Territory and Oregon Country. They also shared scientific descriptions of 122 newly discovered animals and 178 new plants. Americans learned about the climate, soil, mountains, raging rivers, and prairies teeming with beavers and buffalo. They learned about more than fifty Indian nations, including their languages, customs, and potential for trade.

Charles B. J. F. de Saint-Mémin painted this picture of Lewis in 1807 after he returned from the West, wearing the clothes of a frontiersman.

The Lewis and Clark Expedition had mapped huge tracts of Louisiana Territory. The United States also laid claim to Oregon Country based on Lewis and Clark's exploration. Eleven future states—Missouri, Illinois, Kansas, Iowa, Nebraska, South Dakota, North Dakota, Montana, Idaho, Washington, and Oregon—were carved from the lands explored by the Corps.

The expedition crossed 7,689 miles (12,374 km) of wilderness and opened a new frontier for pioneers to settle. Fur trappers, mountain men, and settlers soon headed west. By 1890 the United States stretched from "sea to shining sea." President Jefferson's dream had come true.

NEXT QUESTION

HOW DO WE KNOW SO MUCH ABOUT THE LEWIS AND CLARK EXPEDITION?

Primary Source: Meriwether Lewis's Journal

Seven men in the Corps of Discovery kept journals as they traveled. The five surviving journals are important primary sources of information. A primary source is a document written by a person who was at the place of an event. It is a firsthand description of something that happened long ago. Journals, personal papers, photos, letters, e-mails, and newspapers are examples of primary sources.

Modern-day people can easily learn about the Lewis and Clark Expedition of 1804–1806 by reading primary sources. The following primary source is a portion of Captain Meriwether Lewis's journal entry of April 7, 1805. It describes the day the explorers left the Mandan Indian village and headed west into unexplored territory.

> This little fleet altho' not quite so rispectable as those of Columbus or Capt. Cook were still viewed by us with as much pleasure as those deservedly famed adventurers ever beheld theirs. . . . We were now about to penetrate a country at least two thousand miles [3,220 km] in width, on which the foot of civilized man had never trodden; the good or evil it had in store for us was for experiment yet to determine. . . . I could but esteem this moment of my departure as among the most happy of my life. The party are in excellent health and sperits; not a whisper of . . . discontent to be heard among them, but all act in unison, and with the most perfect harmony.

To learn more about the Lewis and Clark Expedition, study other primary source material such as William Clark's journal and maps, Patrick Gass's journal, Thomas Jefferson's letters, and portraits of Captain Lewis and Captain Clark.

TELL YOUR EXPEDITION STORY

Pretend you are Captain Meriwether Lewis writing in your journal in October 1805. Describe the moment when you first saw the Rocky Mountains towering in the path ahead of you.

WHERE were you standing?

WHAT did you see?

WHEN did you first realize that there was no Northwest Passage across the North American continent?

HOW did you feel?

WHO was with you?

WHY did you go on the expedition?

USE **WHO, WHAT, WHERE, WHY, WHEN,** AND **HOW** TO THINK OF OTHER QUESTIONS TO HELP YOU CREATE YOUR STORY!

Timeline

1803

Emperor Napoleon of France sells the Louisiana Territory to the United States on April 30.

President Jefferson asks Meriwether Lewis to lead an expedition across the West to find a Northwest Passage.

On July 4, President Jefferson announces the Louisiana Purchase.

1804

The United States takes formal possession of the Louisiana Territory on May 10.

On May 14, the Lewis and Clark Expedition begins in Saint Louis, Missouri.

The Corps of Discovery meets the Oto and Missouri Indians on August 3.

In September, the expedition enters the Great Plains where the men see animals unknown in the East, such as buffalo, elk, beavers, jackrabbits, and prairie dogs.

The Corps of Discovery meets the Teton Sioux Indians near present-day Pierre, South Dakota.

On October 24, Lewis and Clark decide to build Fort Mandan across the river from the main village of the Mandan and Hidatsa Indians near present-day Bismarck, North Dakota.

Lewis hires Tousssaint Charbonneau as an interpreter and a cook on November 4. Charbonneau's wife, Sacagawea, joins him.

1804–1805

The expedition winters at Fort Mandan from November to April.

1805

On February 11 Sacagawea gives birth to Jean-Baptiste.

The captains send the keelboat and several men back downriver on April 7, with Indian artifacts, scientific samples, maps, and reports for President Jefferson.

Lewis discovers the Great Falls of the Missouri on June 13.

On August 12, Lewis reaches the Continental Divide on the present-day border of Montana and Idaho.

Lewis finds a Shoshone Indian village and asks for horses to cross the mountains. Sacagawea speaks to the Shoshone chief and discovers that he is her brother, Cameahwait.

The expedition crosses the Rocky Mountains in September.

The expedition reaches the Pacific Ocean on November 15.

1805–1806

The Corps of Discovery winters at Fort Clatsop from December to March.

1806

On March 23, the expedition leaves Fort Clatsop to return home.

The Corps of Discovery splits into two groups. Clark and his group explore the Yellowstone River. Lewis and his men run into Blackfeet Indians near the Marias River.

The expedition returns to the Mandan and Hidatsa villages.

On September 23, the Corps of Discovery reaches Saint Louis, ending the expedition.

After their return, Lewis and Clark travel to Washington, D.C. to report to President Jefferson.

Source Notes

8 Donald Jackson, ed., *Letters of the Lewis and Clark Expedition with Related Documents 1783–1854*, vol. 1 (Urbana: University of Illinois Press, 1978), 61.

13 Bernard DeVoto, ed., *The Journals of Lewis and Clark* (New York: Houghton Mifflin Co., 1953), 28.

14 Stephen E. Ambrose, *Undaunted Courage: Meriwether Lewis, Thomas Jefferson, and the Opening of the American West* (New York: Simon & Schuster, 1996), 206.

20 Gary E. Moulton, ed., *The Lewis and Clark Journals: An American Epic of Discovery* (Lincoln: University of Nebraska Press, 2003), 126.

22 Ibid., 173.

23 DeVoto, 189.

25 Patrick Gass, *The Journals of Patrick Gass: Member of the Lewis and Clark Expedition, ed.* Carol Lynn MacGregor (Missoula, MT: Mountain Press Publishing Co., 1997), 130.

25 DeVoto, 239.

26 Dayton Duncan and Ken Burns, *Lewis & Clark: The Journey of the Corps of Discovery* (New York: Knopf, 1997), 144.

28 DeVoto, 264–265.

28 Moulton, 236.

30 Ibid., 247.

35 Ibid., 316.

36 Ibid., 330.

42 Ibid., 91–93.

Selected Bibliography

Ambrose, Stephen E. *Lewis and Clark: Voyage of Discovery*. New York: National Geographic Society, 1998.

———. *Undaunted Courage: Meriwether Lewis, Thomas Jefferson, and the Opening of the American West*. New York: Simon & Schuster, 1996.

DeVoto, Bernard, ed. *The Journals of Lewis and Clark*. New York: Houghton Mifflin Co., 1953.

Duncan, Dayton, and Ken Burns. *Lewis & Clark: The Journey of the Corps of Discovery*. New York: Knopf, 1997.

Gass, Patrick edited by Carol Lynn MacGregor. *The Journals of Patrick Gass: Member of the Lewis and Clark Expedition*. Missoula, MT: Mountain Press Publishing Co., 1997.

Jackson, Donald, ed. *Letters of the Lewis and Clark Expedition with Related Documents 1783–1854*. Vol. 1. Urbana: University of Illinois Press, 1978.

Moulton, Gary E., ed. *The Lewis and Clark Journals*. Lincoln: University of Nebraska Press, 2003.

Further Reading and Websites

Bial, Raymond. *The Mandan.* Tarrytown, NY: Benchmark Books, 2003. Learn about the history and culture of the Mandan Indians from the year A.D. 1000 to modern times, including their encounter with the Lewis and Clark Expedition.

Blumberg, Rhoda. *York's Adventures with Lewis and Clark: An African-American's Part in the Great Expedition.* New York: HarperCollins Publishers, 2004. In this book, the Lewis and Clark Expedition is seen through the eyes of the slave, York, the only African American to travel with the Corps of Discovery.

Discovering Lewis and Clark
http://www.lewis-clark.org
Day-by-day journal excerpts, natural history, a roster of the Corps of Discovery, and more give a good overview of the expedition.

Johmann, Carol A. *The Lewis & Clark Expedition: Join the Corps of Discovery to Explore Uncharted Territory.* Charlotte, VT: Williamson Publishing, 2003. This book focuses on the history of the expedition and includes crafts, activities, and questions for discussion.

Lewis and Clark across Missouri
http://lewisclark.geog.missouri.edu
This comprehensive site has interactive maps of the Lewis and Clark Expedition and animated virtual travel along the Missouri River.

Lewis and Clark: The Journey of the Corps of Discovery
http://www.pbs.org/lewisandclark/
This site, which complements Ken Burns's film, has Corps of Discovery members' journals, a timeline, and interactive stories and trail maps of the expedition.

The Lewis and Clark Trail Heritage Foundation
http://www.lewisandclark.org
This site about the expedition features a Kids' Page with articles, images, quizzes, puzzles, and games.

Patent, Dorothy Hinshaw. *The Buffalo and the Indians: A Shared Destiny.* New York: Clarion Books, 2006. This book is a detailed study of the American buffalo and its role in the lives of Mandan, Hidatsa, Sioux, and other Indian tribes.

Pringle, Laurence. *Dog of Discovery: A Newfoundland's Adventures with Lewis and Clark.* Honesdale, PA: Boyds Mills Press, 2002. Learn about the adventures of Lewis's dog Seaman.

Ransom, Candice. *Lewis and Clark.* Minneapolis: Lerner Publishing Company, 2003. Learn more interesting details about these extraordinary explorers.

Index

Photo Acknowledgments

The images in this book are used with the permission of: © iStockphoto.com/DNY59, p. 1;
© iStockphoto.com/sx70, p. 3 (top), 9, 10 (top), 16, 21 (left), 22 (right), 33, 36, 39; © iStockphoto.
com/Ayse Nazli Deliormanli, PDA on pp. 3, 43; © iStockphoto.com/Andrey Pustovoy, smart phone on
pp. 4, 11, 21, 30; © Connie Ricca/CORBIS, p. 4 (inset); © iStockphoto.com/Serdar Yagci, backgrounds
on pp. 4-5, 43; © Bill Hauser/Independent Picture Service, maps on pp. 5, 7, 23, 29, 37; © Michael
Haynes- www.mhaynesart.com, pp. 5 (bottom), 6, 19, 20, 22 (left), 24, 29 (left), 40, 44; © Francois
Pascal Simon Gerard/The Bridgeman Art Library/Getty Images, p. 7 (top); © SuperStock, p. 8; © MPI/
Stringer/Getty Images, pp. 10 (bottom), 12; Everett Collection, pp. 11 (inset), 41; Independence National
Historical Park, pp. 13, 28; © Smithsonian American Art Museum, Washington, DC/Art Resource, NY,
p. 14; Karl Bodmer, "Mandan Village," from *Prince Maximillan of Wied's Travels to the Interior of North
America,* 1843-1844, The Newberry Library, p. 15; State Historical Society of North Dakota Museum
Collection, 1985.22, p. 17; © John Clymer, *Hasty Retreat,* courtesy of David J. Clymer and the Clymer
Museum of Art, p. 18; © DEA/G.SIOEN/De Agnostini/Getty Images, p. 21 (right inset); © iStockphoto.
com/Talshiar, GPS on pp. 23, 29; © John Clymer, *Lewis and Clark in the Bitterroots,* courtesy of David
J. Clymer and the Clymer Museum of Art, p. 25; Washington State Historical Society/Art Resource, NY,
pp. 26, 27, 34, 35; © Ron Niebrugge/Alamy, p. 30 (inset); Fort Clatsop National Memorial Collection,
National Park Service, FOCL 000104 Cat No. 698, pp. 31, 45; The Academy of Natural Sciences, Ewell
Sale Stewart Library and the Albert M. Greenfield Digital Imaging Center for Collections, p. 32; © W.
Langdon Kihn/National Geographic Society/CORBIS, p. 38; © David David Gallery/SuperStock, p. 43
(painting).

Front cover: The Granger Collection, New York.
Back cover: Library of Congress Geography and Map Division Washington, D.C (G4126.S12 1807.F5).